THE U.S. COAST GUARD

BY CORINNE J. NADEN
AND ROSE BLUE

Defending Our Country
The Millbrook Press
Brookfield, Connecticut

From Corinne:

*To all the Bennett family in Parma, Ohio, with special love
to Jessica, Dale, Jonathan, Rachel, and Mollie.*

From Rose:

For Stephanie Mandel, one of my favorite young readers.

Cover photos courtesy of the U.S. Coast Guard

All photos courtesy of the U.S. Coast Guard except
p. 20: © Lawrence Migdale/Photo Researchers;
p. 56: UPI/Bettmann Newsphotos.
Illustration on p. 34 by Sharon Lane Holm

Library of Congress Cataloging-in-Publication Data
Naden, Corinne.
The U.S. Coast Guard / by Corinne J. Naden and Rose Blue.
p.   cm.—(Defending our country)
Includes bibliographical references and index.
Summary: Surveys the history, organization, personnel, equipment,
and work of the Coast Guard.
ISBN 1-56294-321-9 (Lib. Bdg.)
1. United States. Coast Guard—Juvenile literature.   [1. United
States. Coast Guard.]   I. Blue, Rose.   II. Title.   III. Series.
VG53.N33   1993
359.9′7′0973—dc20   92-31042   CIP   AC

Published by The Millbrook Press
2 Old New Milford Road, Brookfield, Connecticut 06804

★　★　★

CONTENTS

I

Introduction: On the Move with the Coasties 5

II

What the Coast Guard Does and How It Does It 10

III

Modern Coast Guard Equipment 22

IV

Men and Women of the Coast Guard 31

V

Our Coast Guard Then and Now 44

Important Events in Coast Guard History 59
Books for Further Reading 61
Index 62

★ ★ ★

INTRODUCTION:
ON THE MOVE WITH
THE COASTIES

The date is October 11, 1896. The place is the Atlantic Ocean off Cape Hatteras, North Carolina. The schooner *E.S. Newman*, sailing from Providence, Rhode Island, to Norfolk, Virginia, is hit by a hurricane and loses all its sails. It runs aground near one of the most dangerous stretches of shoreline along the Atlantic coast. The nearest rescue station, at Pea Island, is headed by Richard Etheridge, the first black lighthouse keeper in the service. When he and a crewman think they see a faint signal, they hitch mules to a beach cart and race toward the wrecked ship. They find the captain, his wife and three-year-old child, and eight others clinging to the wreckage. But Etheridge is unable to fire a line to them because of the high seas. He orders his men to tie themselves together with rope and wade out to the wreck. When they reach the survivors, they tie each one to the rope and pull them back to safety.

The date is December 10, 1987. The place is 12 miles (19 kilometers) off the coast of southeastern Alaska, in the Pacific Ocean. Jim Blades and his son Clint are fishing for king salmon. The catch is good, but the waves seem unusually large. One minute they can see

A dramatic U.S. Coast Guard rescue at sea.

land, the next minute a mountain of water towers above their wooden fishing boat, the *Bluebird*. Veteran sailor though he is, Jim is slow to realize that a storm is about to overtake them. When he does, he and Clint put on their orange foam-rubber survival suits and head the boat toward land. But it is too late. A huge wave slaps the *Bluebird* against the rocks and it starts to fill with water.

Jim quickly tunes his radio to Coast Guard channel 16. "Mayday! Mayday!" he calls. Moments later, at the Coast Guard air station in Sitka, helicopter 1486 whips into action. Climbing aboard are a veteran pilot and a copilot. With them are three other crew members. An aviation machinist mate will run the hoist that pulls survivors into the ship. An aviation electronics technician will handle the radio, and Jeffrey Tunks will be the Coast Guard rescue-swimmer.

By the time the chopper crew reaches the *Bluebird,* Jim and his son are floundering in the mountainous waves. They cannot grab the rescue basket that is lowered to them. Tunks jumps into the raging waters. With his help, Jim and Clint are pulled into the chopper. But what about Tunks? Can he make it into the rescue basket alone?

The basket is lowered once again. Somehow Tunks pulls himself in. Just then a great gust of wind nearly spills the chopper into the sea. The rescue basket is dragged across the churning waters at a speed of more than 50 knots. The pilot thinks Tunks has been killed. When the basket is pulled into the helicopter, Tunks falls out. At first he doesn't move. Then, slowly, he shakes his head and gives a thumbs-up sign. Mission accomplished!

The date is winter, 1991. The place is the Saint Marys River. It connects Lake Huron and Lake Superior and forms part of the boundary between Michigan and Ontario, Canada. In the cold gray dawn the 140-foot (42-meter) icebreaker *Katmai Bay* punches its way into the

A Coast Guard icebreaking operation.

frozen river. Aboard are the sixteen-member crew and the skipper, thirty-one-year-old Coast Guard lieutenant Sandra L. Stosz. She is the first woman ever to command a U.S. icebreaker. And she loves her job. "Where else," she asks, "can you take a boat out and hit things on purpose?"

In the northern Great Lakes, the icebreaking season runs from November to May. The job of the *Katmai Bay* is to keep the water channel open to navigation. The icebreaker has a thick steel hull with a propeller that acts like a coffee grinder, chewing up chunks of river

ice. In the off season, Stosz and her crew make training runs and help maintain lighthouses.

The date is today. If the place involves the United States and navigable waters, chances are the Coast Guard is at work. It may be on the Mississippi River, a lighthouse off the rocky coast of Maine, a fuel depot in Delaware, an oil rig near Galveston, Texas, a lonely patrol at the top of the world, or one of countless other places. This is the story of the ''Coasties''—the men and women of the United States Coast Guard.

★ ★ ★

WHAT THE COAST GUARD DOES AND HOW IT DOES IT

Semper paratus! That is the motto of the U.S. Coast Guard (USCG). In Latin it means "Always ready," and that is a perfect description of this smallest of all the U.S. armed forces.

The Coast Guard has an awesome job. It patrols all U.S. coastal waters up to 200 miles (320 kilometers) offshore. It covers inland waterways as well as the high seas. It operates wherever there are U.S. bases—from the Arctic to Antarctica, from the top of the world to the bottom. It handles boating safety, navigation aids, search and rescue, commercial shipping, smuggling, drug trafficking, marine science, and customs and tariffs. In fact, if an incident has anything to do with the law and the water, it involves the U.S. Coast Guard.

The Coast Guard is the U.S. government's main maritime (relating to the sea) agency. Unlike the Army, Navy, Air Force, and Marines, which are part of the Department of Defense, the Coast Guard in peacetime is part of the Department of Transportation. In time of war, however, it becomes a military service under the command of the U.S. Navy. The Coast Guard's top sailor is an admiral, whose title is commandant of the Coast Guard.

This unique federal agency and military force has four main missions. It enforces maritime law. It ensures maritime safety. It protects the environment. And it is always ready to defend national security.

To make its work easier, the Coast Guard is divided into two areas—the Atlantic and the Pacific. Each area is commanded by a vice admiral. The Atlantic vice admiral, based at Governor's Island in New York Bay, supervises everything the Coast Guard does from the East Coast to the Midwest, from the Great Lakes to the Gulf of Mexico and throughout the Atlantic Ocean. The Pacific vice admiral, headquartered at Alameda, on San Francisco Bay, California, watches over the entire Pacific Ocean and the ten most western U.S. states, including Alaska and Hawaii.

The seal of the United States Coast Guard, with the motto *Semper paratus*—"Always ready."

★ Districts

Both the Atlantic and Pacific areas cover a lot of territory. So they are divided into ten districts, six for the Atlantic, four for the Pacific. Each one is headed by a district commander, a rear admiral who is in charge of all Coast Guard work in the district, except for cutters, or vessels, that are more than 100 feet (30 meters) long. Captains of those cutters report directly to the two area vice admirals.

All ten districts carry out all the duties of the Coast Guard, but each is known for certain special jobs as well.

One might say that the First District, with its headquarters in Boston, is in charge of lighthouses. There are certainly a lot of them along the 2,000 miles (3,218 kilometers) of coastline from Maine to New Jersey. This busy district watches over more than nine thousand lighthouses and other navigation aids on the eastern seaboard as well as about one million recreational boats. The work requires three thousand Coast Guard personnel and seven thousand volunteers!

The Second District is busy too, but it's more at home on "ole man river." Its main concern is safety on the Mississippi River and other inland waterways. This is the biggest district in land area. With headquarters in St. Louis, it covers twenty-two states from North Dakota to northern Louisiana and from West Virginia to Wyoming. Writer Mark Twain, himself a nineteenth-century Mississippi River pilot, once said, "There is neither light nor buoy to be found anywhere in these thousands of miles of villainous river." Mr. Twain would be in for a surprise today. The Second District is now the fifth-largest user of buoys and other river aids in the world!

The Fifth District covers the states of North Carolina, Virginia, Maryland, Delaware, and parts of New Jersey and Pennsylvania, with headquarters in Portsmouth, Virginia. This district is known as much

The Coast Guard maintains thousands of lighthouses, as well
as other aids to navigation, along the Atlantic coast.

for its history as for its work. It is said to hold the "heart of the Coast Guard." That is because this region is so rich in the early history of the United States and the challenges of the sea. Some of the settlements, including the lighthouses, date back to the very beginnings of the nation.

An average day is never average for District Seven. It includes only three states—South Carolina and most of Georgia and Florida, with headquarters in Miami. Yet it has the largest number of Coast Guard personnel—4,500—and nearly that many auxiliary members. They must patrol almost 2 million square miles (5 million square kilometers) of waterways, the Coast Guard's largest water area. This district is kept very busy with law enforcement, marine safety, and trailing drug smugglers.

A crewman counts the number of packages of cocaine taken from a drug-smuggling vessel by the Coast Guard's "bayou patrol."

The Eighth District is also after drug smugglers. This is the home of the "bayou patrol." It stretches along the coast of the Gulf of Mexico from western Florida to New Mexico, and then up to the Oklahoma border. Its headquarters are at New Orleans. There are more than 3,500 producing oil wells in the Eighth District. No wonder the Coast Guard is mainly concerned here with keeping oil spills, as well as drugs, out of the Gulf.

Breaking up ice usually worries the Ninth District more than cleaning up oil. It includes more than 6,500 miles (10,458 kilometers) of shoreline along the Great Lakes, from western New York to northern Minnesota. The busy Ninth handles about nine thousand search and rescue cases each year. Its headquarters are at Cleveland, Ohio.

The Eleventh District doesn't have to worry about ice. Located in the Pacific area with headquarters in sunny California at Long Beach, it also includes Nevada, Utah, and Arizona. Caring for the environment is the big Coast Guard concern here, with patrols going as far as 1,000 miles (1,600 kilometers) out to sea.

The Thirteenth District, headquartered at Seattle, patrols a much more rugged coastline. It includes Washington, Oregon, Idaho, and Montana. Lots of search and rescue stations dot these often treacherous waters.

The Fourteenth District, based at Honolulu, Hawaii, is the Coast Guard's "Pacific paradise." Although it watches over the beaches of the Hawaiian Islands, its water duties reach all the way to Korea and Japan.

The northernmost of the ten Coast Guard districts is the Seventeenth, with headquarters at Juneau, Alaska. Patrolling Alaska's rugged coasts is a big, as well as tough, job. The Coast Guard in this district must cover a coastline that is long enough to encircle the world!

★ Work

The practical, day-to-day work of the Coast Guard can be divided into seven areas. By far the biggest and the oldest is enforcement of laws and treaties (ELT). Enforcing maritime laws takes up about half of the Coast Guard's time and nearly 40 percent of its annual budget. ELT means making sure that U.S. ships and those of other nations obey U.S. navigation laws. It's not as simple as it sounds. It means enforcing all federal laws on the high seas or in U.S. waters. It means tracking down smugglers who try to get illegal drugs into the country. It means helping to make sure that the millions of recreational boats in the United States are operated as safely as possible. It means patrolling the country's ports and harbors and overseeing the loading and unloading of dangerous cargoes. It means enforcing conservation laws, fishing rights agreements, and international treaties. It means inspecting and licensing the merchant marine, the commercial shipping fleet of the United States. All of this adds up to a lot of work every day of every month of every year.

The second-biggest chunk of the budget, about 21 percent, goes to aids to navigation, which the Coast Guard builds, places, and maintains. A navigation aid is anything that helps a mariner avoid danger on the water and determine his or her ship's position. It might be a short-range aid, such as a foghorn or a lighthouse. It might be a long-range aid, perhaps a radio beacon or the electronic Loran-C and Omega systems. A ship at sea can determine its position by the electronic beam picked up from a Loran-C station more than 1,000 miles (1,609 kilometers) away. The Omega system is newer than the Loran-C system and has a greater range. In the near future, satellites will be part of the Coast Guard's aid to navigation system.

The third-biggest area of the Coast Guard's work is the one that is most familiar to most people. It is search and rescue (SAR), which

The Coast Guard keeps aids to navigation, such as
this channel marker, in good working order.

gets about 15 percent of the budget. The aim of SAR is to save lives and reduce damage to property wherever distress occurs in the marine environment. In order to do this, the Coast Guard links its land stations, ships, boats, and aircraft into one huge communications network.

The fourth-largest share of the budget—about 9 percent—goes to marine safety. The Coast Guard develops and enforces standards for safe ship design, construction, and operation. It makes sure that U.S. ships operate with the required number of qualified crew members. It is the keeper of merchant marine records, determining who is eligible for sea duty.

Close behind marine safety, with almost 9 percent of the budget, is the growing concern called marine environmental protection. Americans are increasingly worried about the effects of pollutants and the damage caused by spills of oil or hazardous substances, such as the horrendous *Exxon Valdez* oil spill in Prince William Sound, Alaska, in 1989. The supertanker caused the worst oil spill in U.S. history. The result was a cleanup cost that ran into the billions of dollars, partly because the work got started slowly. This prompted the U.S. Congress into action. Before the time of the *Exxon Valdez* incident, oil spills were investigated by an on-the-spot Coast Guard coordinator who determined how bad it was and whether it could be contained without extra help. If the Coast Guard said extra help was needed, several government agencies then had to agree on who was to do what. All that took time. And in the case of the *Exxon Valdez,* it took too much time, and the oil spread.

As a result of the Alaskan oil spill, Congress passed the Oil Pollution Act in August 1990. The new law makes the companies that transport oil more responsible in case of a spill. It calls for cleanup to start as soon as the Coast Guard investigates the accident. It also sets

The Coast Guard's marine environmental protection duties include rescuing wildlife injured by oil spills that have washed up onto U.S. beaches.

up a National Response System, headquartered in Elizabeth City, North Carolina, for Coast Guard strike teams. The Coast Guard will keep an inventory of all federal and private equipment to be used in the event of an oil spill or similar disaster. In addition, new Coast Guard equipment is to be set up at nineteen sites around the country to respond quickly to such trouble.

A radarman on watch. Land-based operations
in the Coast Guard are as important as
those that take place on the water.

Because the Coast Guard becomes a branch of the military in wartime, defense readiness is part of the budget—about 4 percent. The Coast Guard has served in every major U.S. national conflict since 1790. To live up to its motto of *Semper paratus,* it must maintain an effective and trained armed force. As part of that program, the Coast Guard has four combat ratings: fire control technician, gunner's mate, radarman, and sonar technician.

The smallest budget chunk, about 3 percent, is ice operations. In 1965 the U.S. Navy transferred this vitally important service to the Coast Guard. Since then, the Coast Guard has taken over all responsibility for the nation's icebreaking operations. In the North and South Pole regions, this means that the Coast Guard escorts supply ships, collects meteorological data, and carries cargo and supplies to isolated scientific and military installations.

These seven areas of operation keep the Coast Guard busy every minute of every day. Just how busy? A Commandant's Bulletin in 1992 listed the following work done on an "average" day in the U.S. Coast Guard:

Aided 361 people.
Answered calls to 23 oil or chemical spills.
Boarded 90 large vessels.
Completed 154 search and rescue cases.
Found 11 illegal aliens.
Inspected 64 commercial vessels.
Investigated 17 marine accidents.
Saved 16 lives.
Saved $2.5 million in property.
Seized 421 pounds (191 kilograms) of marijuana
    and 165 pounds (75 kilograms) of cocaine.
Serviced 150 navigation aids.

★ ★ ★

MODERN COAST GUARD
EQUIPMENT

The easiest thing to remember about any watercraft used by the Coast Guard is this: If it's shorter than 65 feet (almost 20 meters) long and it floats, it's called a boat. The Coast Guard uses about two thousand boats to do its work—motor lifeboats, rescue boats, port security boats, waterways boats, aids to navigation boats, and all kinds of small, non-standard craft.

If a Coast Guard vessel is 65 feet or longer and able to carry a crew for an extended period on the water, it is called a cutter. The versatile cutter is now and always has been the major operating watercraft of the U.S. Coast Guard. There are currently about 250 cutters in service. The smallest of them is the harbor tug with a crew of six enlisted personnel. Its main missions are search and rescue, ice operations, and responding to pollution spills.

Buoy tenders come in four types. The inland tender, 65–100 feet (20–30 meters), carries one officer and fourteen enlisted personnel. The river tender, 65–115 feet (20–35 meters), operates with up to twenty-two enlisted personnel. Coastal tenders are 133–175 feet (40–53 meters) long, and seagoing tenders, which carry seven officers and forty-five enlisted, are 180 feet (55 meters) long. Tenders are used mainly for search and rescue and short-range aids to navigation.

The next largest cutter is the patrol boat, 82–110 feet (25–33 meters). It carries two officers and as many as fourteen enlisted. The Coast Guard has more patrol boats—over one hundred—than any other type of cutter, and they are used mainly for law enforcement.

Above: The seagoing buoy tender is used for search and rescue and to service aids to navigation. Right: The raider boat, which is a small patrol boat, is used in law enforcement—just as the name implies.

Surface effect ships are also used for law enforcement. They carry one officer and sixteen enlisted personnel and are 110 feet (33 meters) in length.

Icebreaking tugs are 140 feet (43 meters) long and carry three officers and fourteen enlisted personnel. They are used for ice operations and search and rescue.

Medium endurance cutters can carry fourteen officers and up to eighty-seven enlisted personnel. These cutters are 105–270 feet (32–82 meters) in length and are used for law enforcement and search and rescue.

Icebreakers are 290–399 feet (88–121 meters) long. They carry up to thirteen officers and 125 enlisted personnel for their ice operations.

The biggest of the cutters is the high endurance cutter. It has up to twenty officers and 158 enlisted personnel. It is 378 feet (115 meters) long and is used mainly for law enforcement and search and rescue. The Coast Guard has twelve of these huge cutters on active duty.

This huge high-endurance cutter is one of twelve owned and operated by the Coast Guard.

An artist's rendering of Coast Guard Signalman Douglas A. Munro protecting withdrawing Marines at Guadalcanal during World War II. Munro was killed in this rescue operation.

One of these twelve cutters is named for Signalman First Class Douglas A. Munro. During World War II, Munro took part in a daring rescue of American Marines on the island of Guadalcanal in the South Pacific. The Coast Guard was operating amphibious (land and sea) craft for the U.S. Navy, which was battling the Japanese. On September 27, 1942, about two hundred Marines were stranded on the beach with enemy troops bearing down on them. Signalman Munro, in one of a dozen landing craft, took charge of rescuing the surrounded men. He and a petty officer kept firing their machine guns as boat after boat went in to shore for the rescue. Shortly after the last Marine was safely on board, Munro was fatally wounded. The U.S. Navy named a destroyer escort after the brave twenty-three-year-old Coast Guardsman, and he became the only member of the Coast Guard to win the Medal of Honor (the highest military decoration of the United States), which was awarded by Congress after his death.

Besides its cutters and boats, the Coast Guard operates more than two hundred aircraft. They are used for search and rescue and law enforcement. Fixed-wing aircraft, such as the HU-25 Guardian, the Coast Guard's first pure jet, operate from Coast Guard air stations. Helicopters take off from air stations as well as from cutters that are equipped with a flight deck. Copters include the twin-engine HH-65A Dolphin, which is used for rescue operations.

These boats and cutters and aircraft are all part of the modern Coast Guard. But the Coast Guard does have another cutter in its inventory, although it could hardly be called modern. Instead, it is steeped in history, one-of-a-kind, and the pride of the service. This is the *Eagle,* a 295-foot (90-meter) sailing ship that is used as a seagoing classroom for about 175 Coast Guard Academy cadets and instructors.

The *Eagle* bears a proud name that goes back to the beginnings of Coast Guard history. The first *Eagle* cutter was commissioned in 1792. The second took part in battles against the French in the Caribbean Sea from 1799 to 1801, and the third was active during the War of 1812. It was commanded by Captain Fredrick Lee, who was also the skipper of the fourth and fifth *Eagle* cutters, from 1816 to 1829.

A century passed before another *Eagle* joined the Coast Guard. This patrol boat, used to stop rum-running during the days of prohibition in the 1920s and 1930s when liquor was illegal, was the only *Eagle* that was not driven by sail.

A HH-3F rescue helicopter during a recovery exercise.

Today's *Eagle* is number seven. Built in Hamburg, Germany, in 1936 to train naval cadets, the ship, originally named the *Horst Wessel*, became a German troop transport and cargo ship during World War II, with three downed aircraft to its credit. When the war ended with an Allied victory, the ship was taken as a war prize. In 1946 the U.S. Coast Guard sailed the vessel from Germany to New London, and it was commissioned the U.S. Coast Guard cutter *Eagle*.

ABOARD THE *EAGLE*

At one time or another, all Coast Guard Academy cadets sail aboard the *Eagle*. It is on the decks of this cutter and up in the rigging that they learn about their future lives at sea.

The square-rigger *Eagle* is the Coast Guard Academy's seagoing classroom. At full sail, this beautiful white ship can cut through the waters at 17 knots. The hull of the *Eagle* is made of steel that is more than a quarter-inch thick. The weather decks are covered with 3-inch-thick (7-centimeter) teakwood laid over steel.

Cadets must learn the names and uses of the more than two hundred lines that maneuver the *Eagle* through the waters. They must handle more than 20 miles (32 kilometers) of rigging and 20,000 square feet (1,860 square meters) of sail. As underclassmen, they take on the jobs that enlisted personnel normally do aboard ship, such as standing watches at the helms. These are the three huge wood and brass wheels that steer the *Eagle*. As upperclassmen, they assume the leadership jobs that officers usually perform.

The lessons of seamanship and respect for the power of the sea learned aboard the *Eagle* stay with these young cadets throughout their lives.

**THE *EAGLE*, THE COAST GUARD ACADEMY'S
SEAGOING CLASSROOM.**

A helmsman on watch aboard a U.S. Coast Guard cutter.

★ ★ ★

MEN AND WOMEN OF THE COAST GUARD

The Coast Guard is the smallest of the five U.S. military services, with only about 38,000 people on active duty. By far the largest number are enlisted—about 30,000, including approximately 2,300 women. Minorities account for about 14 percent of the corps. The Coast Guard is aiming for an overall 12 percent minority population in the officer ranks and 20 percent in enlisted personnel.

Those who apply for the enlisted ranks must be at least seventeen and not more than twenty-six years of age. A high school diploma is desired. If accepted, the recruit signs up for a four-year duty tour that begins with eight weeks of basic training at Cape May, New Jersey. The course is tough, and about twenty out of one hundred recruits don't make it. Of those who do, most will go on to advanced service schools where they can choose from twenty-eight specialties, including aviation machinist mate, marine science technician, sonar technician, or public affairs specialist.

★ The Academy

Young men and women who want to become officers in the Coast Guard may apply for admission to the Coast Guard Academy, located on the shores of the Thames River in New London, Connecticut.

The American government agreed to establish an academy for the Coast Guard on July 31, 1876. It is the third oldest of the four U.S. military schools. The army's U.S. Military Academy, West Point, New York, dates from 1802; the Naval Academy, Annapolis, Maryland, from 1845; and the Air Force Academy, Colorado Springs, Colorado, from 1954.

The academy for the Coast Guard began as the Revenue Cutter School of Instruction. Its first class of nine cadets started training in May 1877 aboard the schooner *J.C. Dobbin*, operating out of New Bedford, Massachusetts. When the cadets weren't on the *Dobbin*, the young men studied math and science in the loft of a nearby boat company. In 1879 the Revenue Cutter School was closed, and it stayed closed until President Grover Cleveland revived it in 1894.

It wasn't until 1900 that the Coast Guard trainees found a land-based home, at Arundel Cove, Maryland. This is the site of the modern Curtis Bay Coast Guard Yard. The school was moved to Fort Trumbull, New London, Connecticut, in 1910. But Congress didn't seem very interested in a school for the Coast Guard. It refused to pass a bill to train more cadets. By 1914 the Revenue Cutter School had only five students.

Cadets train to become officers at the Coast Guard Academy in New London, Connecticut.

Commissioned Officers *(lowest to highest)*

Rank

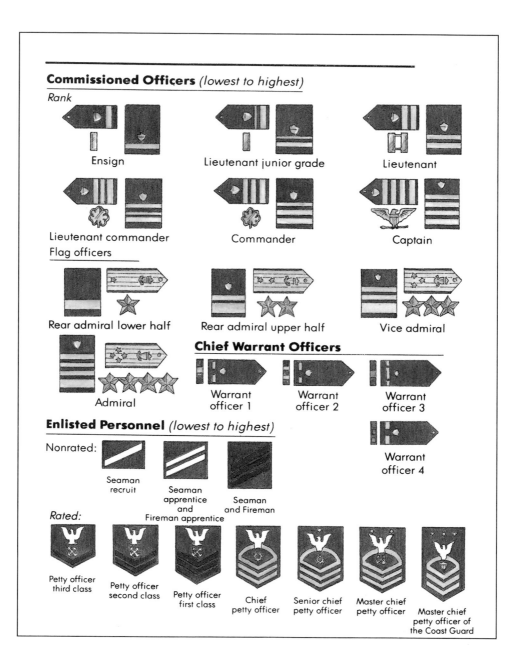

Ensign

Lieutenant junior grade

Lieutenant

Lieutenant commander

Commander

Captain

Flag officers

Rear admiral lower half

Rear admiral upper half

Vice admiral

Admiral

Chief Warrant Officers

Warrant officer 1

Warrant officer 2

Warrant officer 3

Warrant officer 4

Enlisted Personnel *(lowest to highest)*

Nonrated:

Seaman recruit

Seaman apprentice and Fireman apprentice

Seaman and Fireman

Rated:

Petty officer third class

Petty officer second class

Petty officer first class

Chief petty officer

Senior chief petty officer

Master chief petty officer

Master chief petty officer of the Coast Guard

Then along came World War I, and the government became interested again. The Lifesaving Service and the Revenue Cutter Service merged in 1915 to form the U.S. Coast Guard, and the old Revenue Cutter School became the U.S. Coast Guard Academy. When the student body needed more room in 1931, the people of New London donated 110 acres (44 hectares) along the banks of the Thames River. The first of the new buildings on the present site was completed in 1932. The last of the modern expansion program, the Seamanship Sailing Center, was finished in 1984.

Of the four U.S. military academies, the Coast Guard is the smallest, with eight hundred to nine hundred students, and is the only one that admits students based on a nationwide exam. There are no appointments by Congress and no state quotas. To qualify, a young man or woman must be at least seventeen and not yet twenty-two years old, unmarried, and a U.S. citizen. Applications are sent to the director of admissions at the Coast Guard Academy in New London. All candidates must take either the Scholastic Aptitude Test (SAT) or the American College Testing Assessment (ACT). About three thousand students apply each year. Of these, only about three hundred are accepted for each fourth-year, or freshman, class.

Once accepted, an academy freshman must pay a $1,500 entrance fee. For those unable to afford that amount, arrangements are made to deduct money from the cadet's monthly allowance of $543.90 until the fee is paid. Other than the entrance fee, education and training at the academy are free.

As in all U.S. military schools, life in New London is regulated, supervised, and hard. A typical day starts at 6 A.M. with reveille. Classes begin at 8 A.M. and end at 3:45 P.M. There is an hour lunch break. Sports and extracurricular activities fill up the time until the dinner hour at 6:40 P.M. Cadets have free time on the academy grounds until 8 P.M., when study hours start, with taps at 10 P.M.—the end of a long day.

Academy cadets study for a bachelor of science degree in one of seven majors: civil, electrical, or marine engineering; marine, mathematical, or computer science; and government and management. Cadets must all participate in sports as well. All cadets will at various times serve aboard the *Eagle* and other cutters, including a ten-week cruise in their second summer. Part of the academy mission is "to graduate young men and women with sound bodies, stout hearts, and alert minds, with a liking for the sea and its lore, . . ."

All cadets serve aboard the historic cutter
***Eagle* during officer training.**

COAST GUARD TALK

You say . . .	Coast Guard Says . . .
back	aft
bathroom	head
bed	bunk
belongings (clothes, etc.)	gear
Coast Guardsmen	Coastie
dining room	mess hall
floor	deck
forward	fore
get out of bed	hit the deck
goof off	goldbrick
gossip	scuttlebutt
hat	cover
left	port
line up	fall in
meal	chow
right	starboard
room or dormitory	quarters
stairs	ladder
stop	drop anchor
suitcase	seabag
upstairs	topside
wall	bulkhead
yes	aye, aye

**Ribbons and medals are awarded to officer candidates
to indicate certain qualifications or designations,
such as aviation or surface operations.**

In return for their education and training, academy graduates must serve at least six years in the service. They begin military life as ensigns, the lowest naval officer rank. Their first duty is at sea aboard Coast Guard cutters that may be stationed anywhere in the world. They may serve on an icebreaker in the Arctic, a search and rescue patrol along the coast, or a cutter that aids navigation on the Great Lakes. After that first tour of duty, they can apply for aviation training or command of a patrol boat.

Overall, the Coast Guard has about five thousand officers. Most of them—six out of ten—come from the academy. But that isn't the only way to earn a Coast Guard commission. Qualified college graduates or enlisted Coast Guard personnel can apply for admission to officer candidate school in Yorktown, Virginia, and go on to become officers in the U.S. Coast Guard.

★ Women in the Coast Guard

Women have served in the Coast Guard since 1942, when the Women's Reserve was created during World War II. They have been part of the active-duty Coast Guard since 1973, but they were doing Coast Guard work long before that.

In the late 1700s, the U.S. government established a Lighthouse Service to help bring ships safely to the often dangerous eastern shores. Romantic tales were spun of hardy seafaring men bravely spending long lonely hours keeping those on the sea from harm. Actually, the ''hardy seafaring'' lighthouse keeper was often a woman, and the life of a lighthouse keeper was apt to be pretty lively. For one thing, there were quite a few shipwrecks. Many lighthouses were destroyed by hurricanes and storms, and some were attacked by Indians.

Probably the most famous woman lighthouse keeper was Idawally Zorada Lewis. She took care of the Lime Rock Lighthouse in the harbor at Newport, Rhode Island, for thirty-nine years. Only four months after her father was appointed lighthouse keeper, he was taken ill. So Ida, just sixteen at the time, took over the job. Her title was not made official until 1872, when her father died. But by then she was already famous for a number of rescues. President Ulysses S. Grant even made a trip to Newport Harbor to visit her. She is credited with saving eighteen people, the last when she was sixty-five years old and pulled a

Ida Lewis, "the heroine of Newport," as she appeared
on the cover of *Harper's Weekly* in 1869.

drowning woman out of the harbor. Years later, after her death, the lighthouse was renamed the Ida Lewis Lighthouse. It was the only time the Lighthouse Service awarded anyone such an honor.

The U.S. Coast Guard Academy was the first of the military academies to admit women, in June 1976. Women now make up about 15 percent of the Corps of Cadets—the student body of the academy. After graduating, they spend long periods at sea, as do the men. The nearly three hundred women officers of the Coast Guard have the same opportunities as male officers to command vessels or fly aircraft. In fact, the Coast Guard was the first U.S. military service to assign women as commanding officers of armed ships.

Women have served in the active-duty Coast Guard since 1973.

The Coast Guard auxiliary is made up of volunteers
who assist the regular Coast Guard with activities such
as boating safety courses for the public.

★ Reservists and Volunteers

The Coast Guard is a small service with a big job. To do its work effectively, it needs the help of reservists and volunteers.

There are about 12,000 people in the Coast Guard Reserve. These men and women train during peacetime to prepare for active Coast Guard duty in time of war. They participate in monthly drills and two-week annual training periods. The 34,000 volunteers, on the other hand, are part of a nonmilitary auxiliary established by Congress in 1939. These civilians operate on their own time and usually at their own expense. They are experienced boaters or licensed aircraft pilots or amateur radio operators. Their purpose is to aid the Coast Guard by such activities as patrolling during marine events and to promote safety in recreational boating. They teach boating courses and help the Coast Guard in search and rescue missions.

OUR COAST GUARD
THEN AND NOW

On the grounds of the U.S. Coast Guard Academy in New London, Connecticut, is an ivy-covered administration building called Hamilton Hall. A Coast Guard cutter called the *Hamilton* is now, and has always been, on active duty. Both the building and the cutter are named for the man regarded as the father of the United States Coast Guard—Alexander Hamilton.

Hamilton was a young man in his early thirties in 1789 when he became the first secretary of the treasury of the new United States of America. Born in the Caribbean, he studied law at King's College, now Columbia University in New York City. During the American Revolution, Hamilton was an aide to General George Washington. When Washington became the country's first president, he remembered his aide's brilliance in the field of finance.

The young nation certainly needed someone who knew about money. The brand-new United States of America faced a debt of $70 million after the Revolution—a truly staggering sum at the time. So Congress passed the Tariff Act of 1789. It put a tax, or customs duty, on incoming and outgoing goods. Not surprisingly, this made a lot of Americans unhappy. They had just won a long and costly war, fought at least in part over unpopular taxes. Back in 1773, their anger over the tax on tea had resulted in the Boston Tea Party. Now these new U.S. citizens weren't much happier about paying taxes to their government than they had been about paying the British. One way to get around the Tariff Act was to bring in goods without paying—in other words, to smuggle.

Secretary Hamilton realized that the government wouldn't be collecting much money unless smuggling was controlled. So, on August 4, 1790, Congress passed his Revenue Cutter Bill. It established the Revenue Cutter Service as part of the Treasury Department, with a fleet of ten ships and forty officers. These cutters were fast and maneuverable. The first one, the *Massachusetts,* was launched in 1791. The cutters patrolled the waters from Maine to Georgia on the lookout for smugglers.

Their work was hampered by the fact that the government did not budget any money for uniforms for the first crews. Some of the cutter officers wore uniforms from the Revolutionary War and carried their old weapons. They had no special flag, either, so it was sometimes difficult to enforce the law with any authority.

One of the earliest records of a revenue cutter at work describes an incident that took place in 1793 near Brunswick, North Carolina. Captain William Cooke, on the *Diligence,* one of the original ten revenue cutters, seized gold from a French ship that had just captured a Spanish brig off the island of Cuba. The French ship had anchored off the coast of North Carolina for repairs. However, the U.S. government ruled that Cooke's seizure of the gold was illegal, and the money was returned to the Spanish.

**Members of the Revenue Cutter Service
capturing smugglers in the 1790s.**

Despite that setback, the original cutters proved to be a good investment, although Alexander Hamilton did not live long enough to see how his Revenue Cutter Service grew. Brilliant and temperamental, he died in 1804 of a wound received in a duel with his longtime political enemy, Aaron Burr.

One of the most dramatic of all captures by a revenue cutter occurred during the War of 1812. The young United States was fighting with Great Britain again. This time the squabble was over shipping rights and the fact that the British seized men—British citizens and deserters, and some Americans, too—from American ships and forced them to serve in the British Navy. The small American navy of sixteen fighting ships and twelve cutters faced six hundred British warships. On the night of October 4, 1813, off Block Island, Rhode Island, the cutter *Vigilant* captured the British privateer *Dart*. This was an especially important prize because the *Dart* had been responsible for the capture of nearly thirty American merchant ships.

★ At War

Throughout the nineteenth century, the Coast Guard continued to be a military branch in wartime. It battled pirates in the Gulf of Mexico in the early 1820s. It transported troops and supplies in the late 1830s when the U.S. government fought the Seminoles in Florida. And Coast Guard cutters saw action during the Mexican War in the 1840s.

During these years, the Coast Guard also secured its role as protector of U.S. tariff and maritime laws. In so doing, it helped to shape American history. There were many times during the country's early growth years when the states tried to rebel against federal law. This was especially true when it involved collecting taxes. In 1832, for instance, South Carolina declared that it would not pay the tariffs imposed by the U.S. government. South Carolina said the tariffs benefited only those states with manufacturing, and South Carolina was a farm state. President Andrew Jackson sent the cutter *McLane* and others into Charleston harbor to enforce the law. They did. The government and the state of South Carolina came to an agreement on a compromise tax, and peace won out.

But fighting wasn't far behind, in the form of the American Civil War (1861–1865). On April 13, 1861, the war's first shot from the

In 1862, during the Civil War, the cutter *Miami* (center in the painting) landed Northern soldiers at Ocean View, Virginia, leading to the capture of Norfolk by Union troops.

deck of a ship came from the Coast Guard cutter *Harriet Lane* in the waters off Charleston. Under command of the U.S. Navy, as all Coast Guard vessels are in wartime, the *Harriet Lane* fired a shot across the bow of the *Nashville,* which had failed to identify itself. The *Nashville* quickly hoisted the Stars and Stripes. Later, the *Harriet Lane* took part in the Union's first victory of the war, at Cape Hatteras, North Carolina. The cutter was later captured by the South in Texas. Another cutter, the *Miami,* helped to land Northern troops and capture Norfolk, Virginia, on May 11, 1862. Whether in actual combat, transporting troops and supplies, or patrolling ports and waterways, more than fifty vessels of the Revenue Cutter Service took part in the Civil War.

★ Saving Lives

Into the twentieth century, in January 1915, the 125-year-old Revenue Cutter Service merged with the sixty-seven-year-old Lifesaving Service to form a new agency in the Treasury Department. And the official title of U.S. Coast Guard was born.

The Lifesaving Service had started in 1848 to aid ships in distress. There were many shipwrecks along the eastern U.S. coast, especially off Long Island and New Jersey. Stations were set up with boats and ropes and other lifesaving tools. They were manned by Revenue Cutter Service personnel and volunteers. Two years after the service began, a volunteer team in New Jersey rescued all but one of the 202 passengers on the ship *Ayrshire,* which had run aground.

When the life saving teams and the Revenue Cutter Service merged, the new agency had a force of more than 4,000 men and 45 cutters, along with 280 lifesaving stations. The first commandant of the Coast Guard was Captain Ellsworth P. Bertholf. He was head of the Revenue Cutter Service before the merger.

★ Patrolling the Waters

Two years after the merger, in 1917, the United States entered World War I. The Coast Guard put on its military hat once again and became part of the Navy Department. It patrolled the waters off the U.S. and Canadian coasts. Six cutters, five thousand enlisted men, and two hundred officers were sent to Europe. Their job was to protect Allied

A Coast Guard lifesaving team races to
the rescue of a ship in distress.

ships from German submarines. One of the Coast Guard cutters was the *Seneca*. On September 16, 1918, it was making its twenty-sixth convoy trip, this time escorting twenty-one ships to Gibraltar at the gateway to the Mediterranean Sea. Suddenly the British tanker *Wellington* was struck by a torpedo from a German submarine. The *Seneca* fired at the sub and drove it off. Then First Lieutenant Fletcher W. Brown and nineteen Coast Guard volunteers boarded the tanker and tried to keep it afloat. The seas became very rough. Brown ordered everyone off the now sinking tanker except for eleven Coast Guardsmen, five merchant sailors, and himself. The destroyer *Warrington* tried to come to the rescue, but the boilers on the tanker exploded and eleven of the *Seneca's* crew died. All of the crew, living and dead, received the Navy Cross.

★ Protecting Ships

At the end of World War I, the Coast Guard returned to the Treasury Department. In 1939 it was joined by what is the oldest of all the branches that became the Coast Guard—the Lighthouse Service. This was another idea of the brilliant Alexander Hamilton. In 1789, Congress had established the National Lighthouse Service to protect mariners from water hazards.

Early lighthouse keepers, stationed on coastal cliffs or offshore islands, used lamps with whale oil, then kerosene, and finally electricity to keep ships away from rocky shores on foggy days and nights. Cannons, bells, foghorns, and sirens warned of danger.

Lighthouses still operate in the United States, but there are no heroic keepers standing by to pull drowning people from the sea. Today's automated lighthouses, which run on batteries, are tended only occasionally by maintenance crews.

THE LIGHTSHIP NANTUCKET,
STRUCK BY THE PASSENGER
LINER OLYMPIC.

LIGHTSHIPS AT SEA

Some parts of the eastern coast are so rocky and steep that lighthouses simply cannot be built. Instead, beginning in 1820, the government stationed lightships in these areas. This was hazardous duty indeed. Lightships worked by guiding ocean traffic with lights and, in later years, radio-beacon signals. Sailing through fog or storms, huge ocean liners would head straight for the radio beacon. Sometimes they ran right into the lightship. The Ambrose Channel lightship in New York Harbor was hit four times in a little more than half a century.

One of the worst lightship disasters happened off the New England coast in the spring of 1934. The lightship *Nantucket* had been sideswiped by an ocean liner that January. It was quickly repaired and put back on duty about 40 miles (64 kilometers) offshore. Then on a foggy morning in May, it was hit again, this time by the passenger liner *Olympic*. The liner was about seventy-five times larger than the lightship it hit. The *Nantucket* sank in minutes, taking down seven of the eleven crew members.

Ironically, the *Olympic* was the sister ship of the ill-fated liner *Titanic*. Back in 1912 the *Titanic* was advertised as "unsinkable." But on its very first voyage it hit an iceberg in the North Atlantic and went down in four hours.

The last operating U.S. lightship, also called the *Nantucket,* was replaced by a navigation buoy in 1985.

★ Defending the Seas

World War II began for the United States when the Japanese bombed Pearl Harbor, Hawaii, on December 7, 1941. Once again, the Coast Guard became part of the Navy Department.

A Coast Guard cutter was involved in action in the first hours of Japan's surprise attack. The cutter *Taney* was docked at Honolulu Harbor when enemy planes roared overhead just before 8 A.M. The attack caught the American forces completely off guard. Within a short time, 19 U.S. ships were sunk, including 4 battleships and 120 planes. When the second wave of Japanese planes appeared just after 9 A.M., the *Taney* opened fire. The cutter spent most of World War II escorting naval convoys in the Mediterranean Sea and Pacific Ocean. It is credited with shooting down a number of Japanese kamikaze, or suicide, planes.

During the war years, 1941–1945, the Coast Guard grew to a force of more than 240,000. Nearly two thousand lost their lives. The U.S. Coast Guard had three main missions in the war. It patrolled the coasts, mainly looking for enemy submarines. Thousands of women volunteers took over these duties. Another mission was troop transport. The Coast Guard used its own cutters as well as ships of the U.S. Navy to carry men and equipment ashore, from the Pacific to the shores of North Africa. The Coast Guard also patrolled the waters around Greenland and the North Atlantic.

In the midst of World War II, the last of the agencies that make up the modern Coast Guard was added. This was the Bureau of Navigation and Steamboat Inspection Service. Congress had created the Steamboat Inspection Service in 1838 to make the nation's waterways safer. In 1932 it was merged with the Bureau of Navigation, responsible for navigation aids such as charts and buoys, and it became part of the Coast Guard in 1942.

The Coast Guard cutter *Taney*, docked in
nearby Honolulu Harbor, fires at enemy planes
during the Japanese attack on Pearl Harbor.

A Coast Guard landing barge unloads American reinforcements into the surf off the coast of France following the invasion of Normandy in World War II.

World War II ended with an Allied victory, and the Coast Guard went back to the Treasury Department. But it wasn't long before fighting started again, this time in Korea (1950–1953). Coast Guard cutters went on patrol in the Pacific to guard airfields and ports.

A few years of peace followed, but the Coast Guard was back under U.S. Navy control in 1965. Coast Guard Squadron One was formed and sent to Vietnam with its patrol cutters. The squadron became part of Operation Market Time, a naval task force set up to guard the Vietnam coastal waters. In addition, the Coast Guard provided security at port cities, supplied navigation aids, and helped to rescue American and South Vietnamese troops from enemy territory. Fifty-six Coast Guard cutters operated in Vietnam, and seven Guardsmen lost their lives.

★ The Coast Guard Today

When the Coast Guard returned to full peacetime duties once more, it was in a new government department. In 1967 the Department of Transportation was created. Part of its responsibility concerns the safety of U.S. waterways and ports, so it seemed logical to transfer the Coasties. After 177 years in Treasury, the Coast Guard became part of the Transportation Department, where it remains today—in peacetime.

The Coast Guard saw wartime duty during Operation Desert Shield and Operation Desert Storm in the Persian Gulf. Iraq invaded the tiny Middle East country of Kuwait on August 2, 1990. The United Nations ordered Iraq to leave, but its leader, Saddam Hussein, refused. U.S. President George Bush sent warships and troops to the Gulf. When he did, he also sent Coast Guard units to serve on the ships. On August 31 a Coast Guard and Navy team boarded an Iraqi tanker in the Gulf— the first such action of the short war that followed. The Coast Guard provided security at port cities in the region and supervised the loading and unloading of ships. Hundreds of Coast Guard reserves joined the regulars in the Persian Gulf action. That was the first time ever that U.S. Coast Guard reserves had been sent overseas.

A U.S. Coast Guard airplane flies over an oil-well fire in Kuwait during the Persian Gulf War.

When the war in the Gulf ended on February 28, 1991, the Coast Guard reserves went back to their usual jobs, and so did the Coast Guard regulars. Today they are rescuing survivors from a sinking boat in New York Harbor. They are breaking up ice on Lake Michigan, or capturing an illegal drug shipment in the Gulf of Mexico. They are keeping a lighthouse bright off Rhode Island and cleaning up an oil spill in San Francisco Bay. They are warning ships away from the dangerous reefs on Waikiki Beach in Hawaii. It's all in a day's work for the Coasties—*Semper paratus!*

★ ★ ★

IMPORTANT EVENTS IN
COAST GUARD HISTORY

1789	The National Lighthouse Service is established.
1790	Congress passes Alexander Hamilton's bill to establish the Revenue Cutter Service, the beginnings of the Coast Guard.
1791	The first cutter, *Massachusetts,* is launched.
1793	Captain William Cooke in the cutter *Diligence* seizes a French ship off the coast of North Carolina.
1813	During the War of 1812, the cutter *Vigilant* captures the British privateer *Dart* off Block Island, Rhode Island.
1848	The Lifesaving Service is established.
1861	The cutter *Harriet Lane* fires the first shot from a ship during the Civil War.
1862	The cutter *Miami* helps to capture Norfolk, Virginia, during the Civil War.
1915	The Revenue Cutter Service and the Lifesaving Service merge under the name U.S. Coast Guard.

1917	During World War I, the Coast Guard sends all six of its cutters to escort duty in Europe.
1934	The *Nantucket* lightship disaster occurs off the New England coast.
1939	The Lighthouse Service joins the U.S. Coast Guard.
1941	On December 7, 1941, during the Japanese attack on Pearl Harbor, the cutter *Taney* engages enemy planes.
1942	The Bureau of Navigation and the Steamship Inspection Service join the Coast Guard; on September 27, Signalman First Class Douglas A. Munro is killed rescuing Marines at Guadalcanal and becomes the only Coast Guardsman to receive the Medal of Honor.
1950–1953	The Coast Guard goes on patrol in Korea.
1965	The Coast Guard goes on patrol in Vietnam.
1967	The Coast Guard becomes part of the Department of Transportation in peacetime.
1990–1991	Coast Guard units are sent on patrol during Operation Desert Shield and Operation Desert Storm.

★ ★ ★

BOOKS FOR
FURTHER READING

Norman Barrett, *Sailing*. New York: Watts, 1988.

Bernard Brett, *The Fighting Ship*. New York: Oxford, 1988.

John Christopher, *Fine Oceans in Peril*. New York: Macmillan, 1987.

Henry F. Halsted, *Boating Basics*. Englewood Cliffs, N.J.: Prentice-Hall, 1985.

Mollie Keller, *Alexander Hamilton*. New York: Watts, 1986.

David Lambert and Anita McConnell, *Seas and Oceans*. New York: Facts on File, 1985.

Corinne J. Naden and Rose Blue, *The United States Navy*. Brookfield, Conn.: Millbrook, 1992.

G. C. Skipper, *Pearl Harbor*. Chicago: Childrens Press, 1983.

INDEX

Page numbers in *italics* refer to illustrations.

Aircraft, 26
Alameda, California, 11
Alaska, 5, 11, 15
Arizona, 15
Atlantic area, 5, 11, 12

Basic training, 31
Bertholf, Ellsworth P., 49
Blades, Clint and Jim, 5, 7
Bluebird (fishing boat), 7
Brown, Fletcher W., 51
Budget, 16, 18, 20, 21
Buoy tenders, 22, *23*
Bureau of Navigation, 54
Burr, Aaron, 46
Bush, George, 57

Civil War, 47–49, *48*
Cleveland, Grover, 33
Coastal tenders, 22
Combat ratings, 20
Commandant of the Coast Guard, 10

Conservation laws, 16
Cooke, William, 45
Cutters, 22–25, *24*, 45

Dangerous cargoes, 16
Dart (privateer), 47
Defense, Department of, 10
Delaware, 12
Diligence (cutter), 45
Drug smuggling, *14*, 15, 16

Eagle (cutter), 26–28, *29*, *36*
Eighth District, 15
Enlisted personnel, 31
Ensigns, 38
Environmental protection, 11, 15, 18–19, *19*
E.S. Newman (schooner), 5
Etheridge, Richard, 5
Exxon Valdez (tanker), 18

Fifth District, 12, 14
First District, 12
Fishing rights agreements, 16
Florida, 14, 15
Fourteenth District, 15

Georgia, 14
Governor's Island, 11
Grant, Ulysses S., 39
Great Lakes, 7, 9
Guadalcanal, *25, 25–26*
Gulf of Mexico, 15, 47

Hamilton, Alexander, 44–46, 51
Harriet Lane (cutter), 48
Hawaii, 11, 15
Helicopters, 7, 26, *27*
HH-65A Dolphin rescue helicopters, 26
HH-3F rescue helicopters, 27
High endurance cutters, 24, *24,* 25
HU-25 Guardian aircraft, 26

Icebreakers, 24
Icebreaking operations, 7–9, *8–9,* 15, 21, 24
Icebreaking tugs, 24
Idaho, 15
Inland tenders, 22
International treaties, 16

Jackson, Andrew, 47
Juneau, Alaska, 15

Katmai Bay (icebreaker), 7, 9
Korean War, 56

Language, 37
Law enforcement, 11, 16, 23, 24, 47
Lee, Fredrick, 26
Lewis, Idawally Zorada, 39, *40,* 41
Lifesaving Service, 35, 49
Lighthouses, 12, *13,* 14, 39, 41, 51
Lightships, *52, 53*
Long Beach, California, 15
Loran-C system, 16
Louisiana, 12

Maritime safety, 11, 18
Maryland, 12

Massachusetts (cutter), 45
Medal of Honor, 26
Medium endurance cutters, 24
Merchant marine, 16, 18
Mexican War, 47
Miami (cutter), 48
Miami, Florida, 14
Minorities, 31
Mississippi River, 12
Montana, 15
Munro, Douglas A., *25, 25–26*

Nantucket (lightship), *52, 53*
National Lighthouse Service, 39, 41, 51
Navigation aids, 12, 16, *17,* 54
Nevada, 15
New Jersey, 12
New Orleans, Louisiana, 15
Ninth District, 15
North Carolina, 12
North Dakota, 12

Officers, 33, 35–36, 38–39
Oil Pollution Act of 1990, 18
Oil spills, 15, 18–19, *19*
Oklahoma, 15
Olympic (liner), *52, 53*
Omega system, 16
Operation Market Time, 57
Oregon, 15

Pacific area, 11, 12
Patrol boats, 23, *23*
Pearl Harbor, 54
Pennsylvania, 12
Persian Gulf War, 57, *58*
Portsmouth, Virginia, 12
Prohibition, 26

Raider boats, *23*
Recreational boating, 43
Reservists, 43
Revenue Cutter School of Instruction, 33, 35

Revenue Cutter Service, 33, 45–46, *46*, 49
River tenders, 22

Saint Marys River, 7–8
Satellites, 16
Seagoing tenders, 22, *23*
Search and rescue (SAR) operations, 5, *6*, 7,
    16, 18, 24, *50*
Seattle, Washington, 15
Second District, 12
Seminole Indians, 47
Seneca (cutter), 51
Seventeenth District, 15
Seventh District, 14
Sitka, 7
South Carolina, 14
Steamboat Inspection Service, 54
Stosz, Sandra L., 8–9
Surface effect ships, 24

Taney (cutter), 54, 55
Tariff Act of 1789, 44, 45
Tenders, 22–23, *23*
Thirteenth District, 15
Titanic (liner), 53
Transportation, Department of, 10, 57
Treasury, Department of the, 45, 51, 57
Tunks, Jeffrey, 7
Twain, Mark, 12

U.S. Air Force, 10
U.S. Air Force Academy at Colorado Springs,
    33
U.S. Army, 10
U.S. Coast Guard
    budget of, 16, 18, 20, 21
    in Civil War, 47–49, *48*
    combat ratings in, 20
    creation of, 35, 45–46, 49
    districts, 12, 14–15
    drug smuggling and, *14*, 15, 16
    enlisted personnel, 31
    environmental protection and, 11, 15,
        18–19, *19*

U.S. Coast Guard (*continued*)
    equipment, 22–28
    icebreaking operations of, 7–9, *8–9*, 15,
        21, 24
    in Korean War, 56
    language, 37
    law enforcement and, 11, 16, 23, 24, 47
    lighthouses and, 12, *13*, 39, 51
    maritime safety and, 11, 18
    minorities in, 31
    missions of, 11
    navigation aids and, 12, 16, *17*, 54
    officers, 33, 35–36, 38–39
    in Persian Gulf War, 57, *58*
    reservists and volunteers, *42*, 43
    seal and motto of, 10, *11*, 20
    search and rescue operations of, 5, *6*, 7,
        16, 18, 24, *50*
    in Vietnam War, 57
    in War of 1812, 46–47
    women in, 8–9, 31, 39, *40*, 41, *41*, 54
    in World War I, 49, 51
    in World War II, 25–26, 54, *55*, 56, *56*
U.S. Coast Guard Academy at New London,
    28, 33, 35–36, 41
U.S. Marine Corps, 10, 25–26
U.S. Military Academy at West Point, 33
U.S. Naval Academy at Annapolis, 33
U.S. Navy, 10, 25, 26
Utah, 15

Vietnam War, 57
Vigilant (cutter), 47
Virginia, 12
Volunteers, *42*, 43

War of 1812, 46–47
Washington, George, 44
Washington state, 15
West Virginia, 12
Women, 8–9, 31, 39, *40*, 41, *41*, 54
World War I, 49, 51
World War II, 25–26, 54, *55*, 56, *56*
Wyoming, 12